Linear Algebra for Ma
Foundations and Applications

I0019236

Bimal P R Kujur

Preface

Machine learning is revolutionizing industries by enabling computers to learn from data and make intelligent decisions. At the heart of machine learning lies linear algebra—a fundamental mathematical framework that powers algorithms, optimizations, and data transformations. This book, Linear Algebra for Machine Learning: Foundations and Applications, aims to bridge the gap between theoretical concepts and practical applications by providing an intuitive understanding of linear algebra's role in machine learning models.

This book is structured to cater to both beginners and experienced practitioners. It starts with foundational concepts of linear algebra, including vectors, matrices, and eigenvalues, before progressing to their applications in machine learning. Each includes theoretical explanations accompanied by hands-on coding demonstrations to reinforce learning through practical implementation.

By the end of this book, readers will gain a solid grasp of how linear algebra is employed in machine learning algorithms such as Support Vector Machines, Neural Networks, and Principal Component Analysis. The combination of mathematical insights and code demonstrations will equip readers with the skills necessary to develop, optimize, and interpret machine learning models effectively.

Whether you are a student, researcher, or professional, this book serves as a comprehensive guide to understanding and applying linear algebra in the field of machine learning.

Table of Contents

1. SYSTEMS OF LINEAR EQUATIONS FOR TWO VARIABLES

In this Chapter, we'll explore systems of linear equations for two variables, their significance in linear algebra, and practical applications in machine learning. We'll discuss how to solve these systems analytically and programmatically, using Python to demonstrate practical implementation.

Introduction to Systems of Linear Equations

A system of linear equations consists of two or more linear equations involving the same variables. For two variables, a system looks like this:

$$a_1x + b_1y = c_1$$

(1)

$$a_2x + b_2y = c2$$
(2)

Here:

- $a_1, b_1, c_1, a_2, b_2, c_2$ are constants.
- x and y are the variables to solve for.

Geometric Interpretation

Each linear equation represents a straight line in a 2D coordinate plane. The solution to the system is the point(s) where the lines intersect:

- **One solution**: The lines intersect at a single point.

- **Infinite solutions**: The lines coincide (are the same).

- **No solution**: The lines are parallel and do not intersect.

Solving Systems of Linear Equations

There are three common methods to solve a system of equations:

1. **Graphical Method**
   Plot the lines and identify the intersection point (if any).

2. **Substitution Method**
   Solve one equation for one variable and substitute it into the other equation.

3. **Elimination Method**
   Combine the equations to eliminate one variable, then solve for the other.

Example System

Let's consider this system of equations:

$$2x + 3y = 8 \qquad (3)$$
$$x - y = 2 \qquad (4)$$

We'll solve this system step-by-step using Python.

Hands-On: Solving Systems of Linear Equations with Python

Python provides various tools to solve systems of linear equations efficiently. Here, we'll use:

1. **NumPy** for direct computation.

2. **SymPy** for symbolic computation and visualization.

Using NumPy

NumPy is a powerful library for numerical computations in Python. To solve a system of linear equations, we can represent it in **matrix form**:

$$AX = B$$

Where:

- A is the coefficient matrix.
- X is the column vector of variables.
- B is the constant vector.

For our example

$$A = \begin{bmatrix} 2 & 3 \\ 1 & -1 \end{bmatrix}, X = \begin{bmatrix} x \\ y \end{bmatrix}, B = \begin{bmatrix} 8 \\ 2 \end{bmatrix}$$

Let's solve this using Python:

```python
import numpy as np

# Coefficient matrix A
A = np.array([[2, 3], [1, -1]])

# Constant matrix B
B = np.array([8, 2])

# Solving for X
X = np.linalg.solve(A, B)

print(f"Solution: x = {X[0]}, y = {X[1]}")
```

Output:

X = 2.0, y = 1.0

This tells us that the lines intersect at the point (2,1).

Using SymPy

SymPy is a Python library for symbolic mathematics. It's especially useful for analytical solutions and visualizing equations.

```python
from sympy import symbols, Eq, solve

# Define symbols for variables
x, y = symbols('x y')

# Define the equations
eq1 = Eq(2*x + 3*y, 8)
eq2 = Eq(x - y, 2)

# Solve the system of equations
solution = solve((eq1, eq2), (x, y))

print(f"Solution: {solution}")
```

Output:

x=2 , y=1

This output confirms our earlier result.

Graphical Representation

Plotting the lines gives a visual confirmation of the solution. Let's plot using Matplotlib.

```python
import matplotlib.pyplot as plt
import numpy as np

# Define the equations
x_vals = np.linspace(-1, 5, 100)
y1_vals = (8 - 2*x_vals) / 3  # From 2x + 3y = 8
y2_vals = x_vals - 2          # From x - y = 2

# Plot the lines
plt.plot(x_vals, y1_vals, label='2x + 3y = 8')
plt.plot(x_vals, y2_vals, label='x - y = 2')

# Highlight the solution point
plt.scatter(2, 1, color='red', label='Solution (2, 1)')

# Configure the plot
plt.axhline(0, color='black',linewidth=0.5)
plt.axvline(0, color='black',linewidth=0.5)
plt.grid(color = 'gray', linestyle = '--', linewidth = 0.5)
plt.legend()
plt.xlabel('x')
plt.ylabel('y')
plt.title('Graphical Solution of Linear Equations')
plt.show()
```

The plot will show two intersecting lines with a red dot at (2,1)(2, 1)(2,1), confirming the solution.

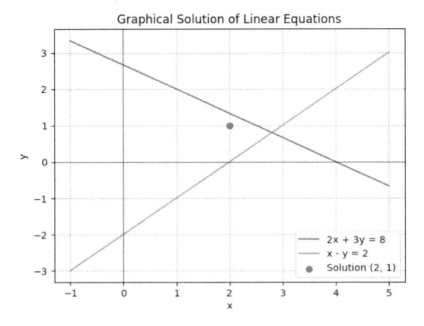

Applications in Machine Learning

Systems of linear equations form the backbone of many machine learning algorithms, particularly in solving optimization problems. Some applications include:

1. **Linear Regression**: Determining the best-fit line for a set of data points by minimizing error.

2. **Support Vector Machines**: Solving for hyperplanes in high-dimensional spaces.

3. **Neural Networks**: Linear transformations in forward and backward propagation.

2. SYSTEMS OF LINEAR EQUATIONS FOR THREE VARIABLES

In this Chapter , we'll extend our understanding of systems of linear equations to three variables. We'll cover analytical approaches, visualization, and computational methods for solving these systems using Python. This topic forms a crucial foundation for machine learning tasks that rely on multidimensional linear algebra concepts.

Introduction to Systems of Linear Equations with Three Variables

A **system of linear equations with three variables** consists of equations in the following form:

$$a_1x + b_1y + c_1z = d_1 \qquad (1)$$

$$a_2x + b_2y + c_2z = d_2 \qquad (2)$$

$$a_3x + b_3y + c_3z = d_3 \qquad (3)$$

Here:

- $a_1, b_1, c_1, d_1, a_2, b_2, c_2, d_2, a_3, b_3, c_3, d_3$ are constants.
- x, y, z are the variables to solve for.

Geometric Interpretation

In a three-dimensional space, each equation represents a plane. The solution to the system is the point(s) where these planes intersect:

- **One solution**: The planes intersect at a single point.

- **Infinite solutions**: The planes intersect along a line or overlap completely.

- **No solution**: The planes do not intersect (e.g., they are parallel or form a triangular prism).

Methods for Solving Systems of Three Variables

The system can be solved using the following methods:

1. **Substitution Method**
   Solve one equation for one variable and substitute into the other equations.

2. **Elimination Method**
   Eliminate variables by adding or subtracting equations to isolate the remaining variables.

3. **Matrix Method**
   Represent the system in matrix form and solve using computational tools (e.g., NumPy).

Example System

Consider this system of equations:

$x + y + z = 6$ (4)

$2x - y + z = 3$ (5)

$x - 2y + 3z = 14$ (6)

Let's solve it using Python.

Hands-On: Solving Systems of Three Variables with Python

Using NumPy

The system can be written in matrix form:

$$AX = B$$

Where:

$$A = \begin{bmatrix} 1 & 1 & 1 \\ 2 & -1 & 1 \\ 1 & -2 & 3 \end{bmatrix}, X = \begin{bmatrix} x \\ y \\ z \end{bmatrix}, B = \begin{bmatrix} 6 \\ 3 \\ 14 \end{bmatrix}$$

Using NumPy, we can solve this system efficiently.

```
import numpy as np

# Coefficient matrix A
A = np.array([[1, 1, 1],
              [2, -1, 1],
              [1, -2, 3]])

# Constant matrix B
B = np.array([6, 3, 14])

# Solve for X
X = np.linalg.solve(A, B)

print(f"Solution: x = {X[0]}, y = {X[1]}, z = {X[2]}")
```

Output:

X = 3.0, y = 1.0, z = 2.0

This tells us that the planes intersect at the point (3,1,2).

Using SymPy

SymPy allows for symbolic computation, which is useful for analytical solutions.

```
from sympy import symbols, Eq, solve

# Define symbols for variables
x, y, z = symbols('x y z')

# Define the equations
eq1 = Eq(x + y + z, 6)
eq2 = Eq(2*x - y + z, 3)
eq3 = Eq(x - 2*y + 3*z, 14)

# Solve the system of equations
solution = solve((eq1, eq2, eq3), (x, y, z))

print(f"Solution: {solution}")
```

Output:

X = 3, y = 1, z = 2

Graphical Representation

While it is challenging to visualize three planes in 3D space on a 2D medium, we can plot their intersection using Matplotlib's 3D plotting tools.

```
# Define the planes
x_vals = np.linspace(-1, 5, 30)
y_vals = np.linspace(-1, 5, 30)
x, y = np.meshgrid(x_vals, y_vals)

# Plane equations
z1 = 6 - x - y        # From x + y + z = 6
z2 = 3 - 2*x + y      # From 2x - y + z = 3
z3 = (14 - x + 2*y) / 3  # From x - 2y + 3z = 14

# Create the 3D plot
fig = plt.figure()
ax = fig.add_subplot(111, projection='3d')

# Plot the planes
ax.plot_surface(x, y, z1, alpha=0.5, rstride=100, cstride=100, color='red', label='Plane 1')
ax.plot_surface(x, y, z2, alpha=0.5, rstride=100, cstride=100, color='blue', label='Plane 2')
ax.plot_surface(x, y, z3, alpha=0.5, rstride=100, cstride=100, color='green', label='Plane 3')

# Plot the solution point
ax.scatter(3, 1, 2, color='black', s=50, label='Solution (3, 1, 2)')

# Configure the plot
ax.set_xlabel('X-axis')
ax.set_ylabel('Y-axis')
ax.set_zlabel('Z-axis')
plt.title('Intersection of Three Planes')
plt.legend()
plt.show()
```

Intersection of Three Planes

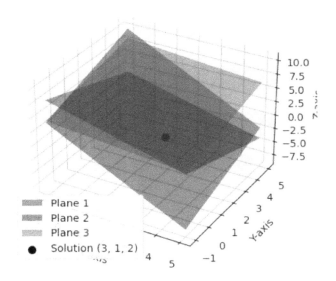

Applications in Machine Learning

Systems of linear equations with three or more variables frequently appear in machine learning tasks, particularly in:

1. **Multivariable Linear Regression**: Solving for coefficients when predicting an output based on multiple features.

2. **Optimization Problems**: Constrained optimization often involves solving systems of equations.

3. **Dimensionality Reduction**: Techniques like PCA rely on solving eigenvalue problems derived from linear systems.

3. SOLVING SYSTEMS OF LINEAR EQUATIONS

Solving systems of linear equations is a cornerstone of linear algebra, with applications spanning data analysis, machine learning, and optimization. This explores various methods to solve systems of equations, their relevance in machine learning, and Python-based implementations for both small and large systems.

Introduction to Systems of Linear Equations

A **system of linear equations** consists of multiple linear equations that share the same set of variables. Mathematically, a system of nnn equations with nnn variables can be represented as:

$$a_{1,1}x_1 + a_{1,2}x_2 + \cdots + a_{1,n}x_n = b_1 \qquad (1)$$

$$a_{2,1}x_1 + a_{2,2}x_2 + \cdots + a_{2,n}x_n = b_2 \qquad (2)$$

$$\vdots \qquad\qquad \vdots \qquad\qquad \vdots$$

$$\vdots \qquad\qquad \vdots \qquad\qquad \vdots$$

$$\vdots \qquad\qquad \vdots \qquad\qquad \vdots$$

$$a_{n,1}x_1 + a_{n,2}x_2 + \cdots + a_{n,n}x_n = b_n \qquad (n)$$

Here:

- $a_{i,j}$ are the coefficients of the variables, forming the coefficient matrix A.

- b_i are the constants forming the result vector B.
- $X_1, X_2, \ldots, X_n$ are the variables to solve for, forming the solution vector X.

Matrix Representation

Systems of linear equations can be written concisely in **matrix form**:

AX = B

Where:

- A is the n×n coefficient matrix.
- X is the n×1 solution vector.
- B is the n×1 result vector.

For example, consider the system:

2x + 3y = 8   (3)

x − 2y = −3   (4)

This can be written as:

$$A = \begin{bmatrix} 2 & 3 \\ 1 & -2 \end{bmatrix}, X = \begin{bmatrix} x \\ y \end{bmatrix}, B = \begin{bmatrix} 8 \\ -3 \end{bmatrix}$$

The solution X can be obtained by solving AX = B.

Methods for Solving Systems of Linear Equations

Several methods exist for solving systems of linear equations, including:

1. **Substitution and Elimination Methods**: Useful for small systems but inefficient for large systems.
2. **Matrix Methods**: Use linear algebra concepts like inverses, determinants, or computational tools.

3. **Iterative Methods**: Suitable for large systems, e.g., gradient descent and Jacobi methods.

Direct Methods

- **Gaussian Elimination**: Reduces the system to row echelon form.

- **LU Decomposition**: Factors the coefficient matrix into a product of lower and upper triangular matrices.

- **Matrix Inversion**: Solves $X = A^{-1}B$ (only if A is invertible).

Hands-On: Solving Systems of Linear Equations with Python

Python provides robust tools like **NumPy** and **SymPy** for solving systems of equations efficiently. Let's explore them through examples.

Example 1: Solving a 2x2 System with NumPy

Consider the system:

$$2x + 3y = 8 \qquad (5)$$
$$x - 2y = -3 \qquad (6)$$

We'll solve this using NumPy's linalg.solve.

```
import numpy as np

# Coefficient matrix A
A = np.array([[2, 3],
              [1, -2]])

# Constant vector B
B = np.array([8, -3])

# Solve for X
X = np.linalg.solve(A, B)

print(f"Solution: x = {X[0]}, y = {X[1]}")
```

Output:

$$x = 1.0, y = 2.0$$

Example 2: Solving a 3x3 System with NumPy

Consider a system of three equations:

$$x + y + z = 6 \quad (7)$$

$$2x - y + z = 3 \quad (8)$$

$$x - 2y + 3z = 14 \quad (9)$$

```
# Coefficient matrix A
A = np.array([[1, 1, 1],
              [2, -1, 1],
              [1, -2, 3]])

# Constant vector B
B = np.array([6, 3, 14])

# Solve for X
X = np.linalg.solve(A, B)

print(f"Solution: x = {X[0]}, y = {X[1]}, z = {X[2]}")
```

Output:

x = 3.0, y = 1.0, z = 2.

Example 3: Symbolic Solution Using SymPy

SymPy allows for symbolic computation, enabling analytical solutions and symbolic manipulation.

```
from sympy import symbols, Eq, solve

# Define symbols for variables
x, y, z = symbols('x y z')

# Define equations
eq1 = Eq(2*x + 3*y, 8)
eq2 = Eq(x - 2*y, -3)

# Solve the system
solution = solve((eq1, eq2), (x, y))

print(f"Solution: {solution}")
```

Output:

x = 1, y = 2

Example 4: Verifying Solutions

It's often useful to verify solutions programmatically, especially for larger systems.

```
# Verify the solution for the 3x3 system
A = np.array([[1, 1, 1],
              [2, -1, 1],
              [1, -2, 3]])
B = np.array([6, 3, 14])

# Computed solution
X = np.linalg.solve(A, B)

# Verify by substituting into AX = B
verification = np.allclose(np.dot(A, X), B)
print(f"Solution verified: {verification}")
```

Output:

Solution verified: True\text{Solution verified: True} Solution verified: True

Applications in Machine Learning

1. **Linear Regression**
   Solving systems of linear equations is fundamental for fitting a linear model to data. For example, in simple linear regression, the normal equation:

$$\Theta =$$

$(X^TX)^{-1}X^Ty$

is solved using matrix operations.

2. **Optimization**
   Many machine learning algorithms involve

minimizing a loss function, which often boils down to solving a system of equations (e.g., gradient equations).

3. **Feature Transformation**
   Linear transformations, such as PCA, involve solving eigenvalue problems, which are systems of equations in disguise.

4. FINDING RANK OF A MATRIX VIA ROW ECHELON FORM

In this part, we will explore how to find the rank of a matrix using the **row echelon form**. The concept of rank is crucial in linear algebra and machine learning because it helps identify the dimensionality of data, determine the solvability of systems of linear equations, and more. We'll explain the mathematical intuition, algorithmic approach, and demonstrate Python implementations to compute the rank.

What is the Rank of a Matrix?

The **rank** of a matrix is the maximum number of linearly independent rows (or columns) in the matrix. Intuitively, it represents the amount of unique information or the dimensionality of the vector space spanned by the rows or columns of the matrix.

Key Points:

1. **Full Rank**: A matrix is full rank if its rank equals the smaller of the number of rows or columns.

2. **Rank Deficiency**: If a matrix has dependent rows or columns, its rank is less than the total number

of rows or columns.

3. **Applications**: Rank is used to:
   - Determine if a system of linear equations has a unique solution.
   - Analyze the dimensionality of feature spaces in machine learning.

Row Echelon Form

The **row echelon form** (REF) of a matrix is a triangularized version where the following properties hold:

1. The first non-zero element (pivot) in each row is to the right of the pivot in the row above it.

2. Rows with all zeros are at the bottom of the matrix.

For example, the row echelon form of a matrix might look like this:

$$\begin{bmatrix} 1 & 2 & 3 \\ 0 & 1 & 4 \\ 0 & 0 & 1 \end{bmatrix}$$

Rank via Row Echelon Form:

The rank of a matrix is equal to the number of non-zero rows in its row echelon form.

Algorithm for Row Echelon Form

1. **Identify the Pivot**: Find the first non-zero element in each row (the pivot).

2. **Eliminate Below**: Use the pivot to make all elements below it zero by row operations.

3. **Move Right**: Move to the next row and repeat the process.

4. **Count Non-Zero Rows**: Once the matrix is in row echelon form, count the rows with at least one

non-zero element.

Hands-On: Finding Rank Using Python

Let's compute the rank of a matrix using Python. We'll demonstrate three approaches:

1. Manual computation using row echelon form.
2. Using **NumPy** for built-in rank computation.
3. Using **SymPy** for symbolic row reduction.

Example Matrix

Consider the following matrix:

$$A = \begin{bmatrix} 2 & 4 & 1 \\ 6 & 12 & 4 \\ 10 & 20 & 7 \end{bmatrix}$$

Manual Row Reduction to Row Echelon Form

```python
import numpy as np

def row_echelon_form(matrix):
    """Converts a matrix to Row Echelon Form and returns it."""
    m = matrix.astype(float)  # Ensure calculations are in float
    rows, cols = m.shape
    pivot_row = 0

    for col in range(cols):
        # Find the pivot row
        max_row = pivot_row + np.argmax(abs(m[pivot_row:, col]))
        if m[max_row, col] == 0:
            continue  # No pivot in this column

        # Swap the pivot row with the current row
        m[[pivot_row, max_row]] = m[[max_row, pivot_row]]

        # Normalize the pivot row
        m[pivot_row] = m[pivot_row] / m[pivot_row, col]

        # Eliminate rows below the pivot
        for row in range(pivot_row + 1, rows):
            m[row] -= m[row, col] * m[pivot_row]

        pivot_row += 1

    return m

def rank_from_row_echelon(matrix):
    """Finds the rank of a matrix by counting non-zero rows in its row echelon form."""
    row_echelon = row_echelon_form(matrix)
    return np.sum(~np.all(row_echelon == 0, axis=1))

# Define the matrix
A = np.array([[2, 4, 1],
              [6, 12, 4],
              [10, 20, 7]])

# Compute Row Echelon Form and Rank
row_echelon = row_echelon_form(A)
rank = rank_from_row_echelon(A)

print("Row Echelon Form of A:")
print(row_echelon)
print(f"Rank of A: {rank}")
```

Output:

Row Echelon Form of A:

$$A = \begin{bmatrix} 1 & 2 & 0.5 \\ 0 & 0 & 1 \\ 0 & 0 & 0 \end{bmatrix} \quad ; \text{Rank of A: 2}$$

Using NumPy's Built-In Rank Function

```python
import numpy as np

# Define the matrix
A = np.array([[2, 4, 1],
              [6, 12, 4],
              [10, 20, 7]])

# Compute the rank using NumPy
rank = np.linalg.matrix_rank(A)

print(f"Rank of A: {rank}")
```

Output:

Rank of A: 2

NumPy automatically calculates the rank by determining the number of singular values that are non-zero.

Using SymPy for Symbolic Row Reduction

```python
from sympy import Matrix

# Define the matrix
A = Matrix([[2, 4, 1],
            [6, 12, 4],
            [10, 20, 7]])

# Compute the row echelon form and rank
row_echelon, pivots = A.rref()
rank = A.rank()

print("Row Echelon Form of A:")
print(row_echelon)
print(f"Rank of A: {rank}")
```

Output:

Row Echelon Form of A:

$$\begin{bmatrix} 1 & 2 & 0.5 \\ 0 & 0 & 1 \\ 0 & 0 & 0 \end{bmatrix}$$

Rank of A: 2

SymPy provides both the row echelon form (rref) and the rank of the matrix.

Applications of Rank in Machine Learning

1. **Feature Selection and Dimensionality Reduction**
   - Rank identifies the true dimensionality of data, helping reduce redundant or collinear features.

2. **Solvability of Linear Systems**
   - A system of linear equations has a solution if the rank of the coefficient matrix equals the rank of the augmented matrix.

3. **Principal Component Analysis (PCA)**
   - PCA involves decomposing data into orthogonal components, where rank determines the number of principal components.

5. VECTORS AND LINEAR TRANSFORMATIONS

Vectors and linear transformations are fundamental concepts in linear algebra that underpin many areas of machine learning, including data representation, feature transformation, and model optimization. This introduces vectors, explains the concept of linear transformations, and provides practical Python demonstrations for better understanding.

What is a Vector?

A **vector** is a mathematical object that represents a quantity with both **magnitude** and **direction**. In machine learning, vectors are used to represent features, weights, gradients, and more.

Key Properties of Vectors:

1. **Dimension**: A vector's size (number of components). For example, $v = [v_1, v_2, v_3]$ is a 3D vector.

2. **Addition**: Vectors can be added component-wise.

$$u + v = [u_1 + v_1, u_2 + v_2, \ldots]$$

3. **Scalar Multiplication**: Multiplying a vector by a scalar scales its magnitude.

$$c \cdot v = [c \cdot v_1,$$

$c \cdot v_2, \dots \dots]$

4. **Dot Product**: Measures similarity between two vectors.

$u \cdot v = \sum u_i v_i$

What is a Linear Transformation?

A **linear transformation** is a function that maps vectors from one space to another while preserving vector addition and scalar multiplication. Mathematically, a transformation TTT is linear if:

$$T(au + bv) = aT(u) + bT(v)$$

Examples of Linear Transformations:

1. **Scaling**: $T(v) = c \cdot v$

2. **Rotation**: Rotating vectors in a plane.

3. **Reflection**: Reflecting vectors across an axis.

4. **Projection**: Projecting vectors onto a subspace.

Linear transformations are often represented by **matrices**:

$$T(x) = A \cdot x$$

Where A is the transformation matrix, and x is the input vector.

Matrix Representation of Linear Transformations

A matrix **A** can transform a vector **x** into a new vector **y**:

$$y = A \cdot x$$

For example:

$$A = \begin{bmatrix} 2 & 0 \\ 0 & 3 \end{bmatrix}, x = \begin{bmatrix} 1 \\ 1 \end{bmatrix}$$

$$y = \begin{bmatrix} 2 & 0 \\ 0 & 3 \end{bmatrix} \cdot \begin{bmatrix} 1 \\ 1 \end{bmatrix} = \begin{bmatrix} 2 \\ 3 \end{bmatrix}$$

This scales the vector by 2 along the x-axis and by 3 along the y-axis.

Hands-On: Vectors and Linear Transformations with Python

Let's implement these concepts using Python.

Example 1: Vector Operations

```python
import numpy as np

# Define vectors
u = np.array([1, 2])
v = np.array([3, 4])

# Vector addition
add_result = u + v

# Scalar multiplication
scalar_result = 2 * u

# Dot product
dot_product = np.dot(u, v)

print(f"Vector u: {u}")
print(f"Vector v: {v}")
print(f"Vector addition: {add_result}")
print(f"Scalar multiplication (2 * u): {scalar_result}")
print(f"Dot product of u and v: {dot_product}")
```

Output:

Vector addition: [4, 6]

Scalar multiplication: [2, 4]

Dot product: 11

Example 2: Matrix Representation of Linear Transformations

We'll apply a scaling transformation to a vector.

```python
# Define the transformation matrix
A = np.array([[2, 0],
              [0, 3]])

# Define the vector
x = np.array([1, 1])

# Apply the linear transformation
y = np.dot(A, x)

print(f"Transformation matrix A:\n{A}")
print(f"Vector x: {x}")
print(f"Transformed vector y: {y}")
```

Output:

Transformation matrix A: $\begin{bmatrix} 2 & 0 \\ 0 & 3 \end{bmatrix}$

Vector x: $[1, 1]$

Transformed vector y: $[2, 3]$

Example 3: Visualizing Linear Transformations

We'll visualize the effect of a matrix transformation on a set of vectors.

```python
import matplotlib.pyplot as plt

# Define the transformation matrix
A = np.array([[2, 0],
              [1, 1]])

# Define the original vectors
vectors = np.array([[1, 0], [0, 1]]) # Basis vectors
transformed_vectors = np.dot(A, vectors.T).T  # Apply transformation

# Plot the original and transformed vectors
origin = np.zeros((2, 2)) # Origin points for vectors
plt.quiver(*origin.T, vectors[:, 0], vectors[:, 1], color=['r', 'b'], angles='xy', scale_units='xy', scale=1, label='Original vectors')
plt.quiver(*origin.T, transformed_vectors[:, 0], transformed_vectors[:, 1], color=['g', 'y'], angles='xy', scale_units='xy', scale=1, label='Transformed Vectors')

# Configure the plot
plt.xlim(-1, 3)
plt.ylim(-1, 3)
plt.axhline(0, color='black', linewidth=0.5)
plt.axvline(0, color='black', linewidth=0.5)
plt.grid(color='gray', linestyle='--', linewidth=0.5)
plt.legend()
plt.title("Linear Transformation of Vectors")
plt.show()
```

This plot will show how the transformation matrix A= $\begin{bmatrix} 2 & 0 \\ 1 & 1 \end{bmatrix}$

scales and skews the original vectors.

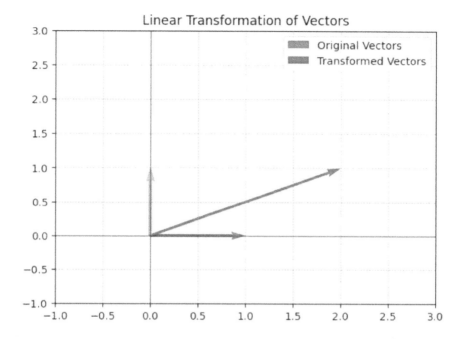

Applications in Machine Learning

1. **Feature Scaling**: Transforming feature vectors for uniformity.

2. **Dimensionality Reduction**: Principal Component Analysis (PCA) projects data onto lower-dimensional spaces using linear transformations.

3. **Neural Networks**: Layers of neural networks involve transformations of input vectors using weight matrices.

4. **Rotation and Projection**: Techniques like SVM kernels project data into higher-dimensional spaces.

BIMAL KUJUR

6. DETERMINANTS AND EIGENVECTORS

Determinants and eigenvectors are fundamental concepts in linear algebra with powerful applications in machine learning. Determinants help us understand matrix properties, such as invertibility, while eigenvectors play a central role in dimensionality reduction, feature extraction, and data transformations. This delves into the mathematics of these concepts and demonstrates how to compute and apply them using Python.

Determinants

What is a Determinant?

The **determinant** is a scalar value that describes certain properties of a square matrix. It is often used to:

1. Determine whether a matrix is invertible ($\det(A) \neq 0$)

2. Measure the scaling factor of a transformation represented by the matrix.

3. Check linear independence of rows or columns in a matrix.

Computing the Determinant

For a 2x2 matrix:

$$A = \begin{bmatrix} a & b \\ c & d \end{bmatrix}$$

The determinant is given by:

$$\det (A) = ad - bc$$

For larger matrices, the determinant is computed using recursive expansion (Laplace expansion) or optimized algorithms.

Properties of Determinants:
1. If $\det(A)=0$, the matrix A is singular (non-invertible).
2. $\det(A^T) = \det(A)$
3. For two matrices A and B: $\det(AB) = \det(A) \cdot \det(B)$

Python Implementation: Determinants

Let's compute the determinant of a matrix using Python.

```python
import numpy as np

# Define a matrix
A = np.array([[3, 1],
              [2, 4]])

# Compute the determinant
det_A = np.linalg.det(A)

print(f"Matrix A:\n{A}")
print(f"Determinant of A: {det_A}")
```

Output:

$$\text{Matrix A: } \begin{bmatrix} 3 & 1 \\ 2 & 4 \end{bmatrix}$$

Determinant of A: 10.0

Eigenvectors and Eigenvalues

What Are Eigenvectors and Eigenvalues?

Eigenvectors and eigenvalues provide insights into how a matrix transforms vectors. For a square matrix **A**, a non-zero vector **v** is an eigenvector if:

$$A \cdot \mathbf{v} = \lambda \cdot \mathbf{v}$$

Here:

- λ is the **eigenvalue**, representing the scalar factor by which the eigenvector is scaled.

- v is the **eigenvector**, representing a direction that remains unchanged (except for scaling) under the transformation A.

Key Properties:

1. The eigenvalues of A are the roots of its **characteristic equation**:

$$\det(A - \lambda I) = 0$$

2. A matrix has as many eigenvalues as its dimension (counting multiplicities).

3. Eigenvectors are useful in understanding the structure and behavior of a matrix.

Applications in Machine Learning:

1. **Principal Component Analysis (PCA)**: Eigenvectors define the principal axes of data.

2. **Spectral Clustering**: Eigenvalues and eigenvectors of a graph's Laplacian matrix help find clusters.

3. **Stability Analysis**: In dynamical systems, eigenvalues help analyze system behavior.

Python Implementation: Eigenvectors and Eigenvalues

Let's compute eigenvalues and eigenvectors using Python.

Example 1: 2x2 Matrix

```python
# Define a matrix
A = np.array([[4, 2],
              [1, 3]])

# Compute eigenvalues and eigenvectors
eigenvalues, eigenvectors = np.linalg.eig(A)

print(f"Matrix A:\n{A}")
print(f"Eigenvalues of A: {eigenvalues}")
print(f"Eigenvectors of A:\n{eigenvectors}")
```

Output:

Matrix A: $\begin{bmatrix} 4 & 2 \\ 1 & 3 \end{bmatrix}$

Eigenvalues of A: [5.0, 2.0]

Eigenvectors of A: $\begin{bmatrix} 0.894 & 0.707 \\ 0.447 & 0.707 \end{bmatrix}$

Each column of the eigenvector matrix corresponds to an eigenvector.

Verifying the Eigenvector-Eigenvalue Relationship

We can verify that $A \cdot \mathbf{v} = \lambda \cdot \mathbf{v}$

```python
# Verify the eigenvector-eigenvalue relationship
for i in range(len(eigenvalues)):
    eigenvalue = eigenvalues[i]
    eigenvector = eigenvectors[:, i]
    result = np.dot(A, eigenvector)
    print(f"Eigenvalue: {eigenvalue}")
    print(f"A @ Eigenvector: {result}")
    print(f"λ * Eigenvector: {eigenvalue * eigenvector}")
    print("-" * 30)
```

This will confirm that the relationship holds for each eigenvector and eigenvalue pair.

Visualizing Eigenvectors

We'll visualize how a matrix transformation affects eigenvectors.

```
import matplotlib.pyplot as plt

# Define a transformation matrix
A = np.array([[4, 2],
              [1, 3]])

# Define eigenvalues and eigenvectors
eigenvalues, eigenvectors = np.linalg.eig(A)

# Plot the original and transformed eigenvectors
origin = np.zeros((2, 2))  # Origin point for vectors
plt.quiver(*origin.T, eigenvectors[0, :], eigenvectors[1, :], color=['r', 'b'], angles='xy', scale_units='xy', scale=1, label='Eigenvectors')

# Apply the transformation
transformed_vectors = np.dot(A, eigenvectors)
plt.quiver(*origin.T, transformed_vectors[0, :], transformed_vectors[1, :], color=['g', 'y'], angles='xy', scale_units='xy', scale=1, label='Transformed Vectors')

# Configure the plot
plt.axhline(0, color='black', linewidth=0.5)
plt.axvline(0, color='black', linewidth=0.5)
plt.xlim(-1, 6)
plt.ylim(-1, 6)
plt.grid(color='gray', linestyle='--', linewidth=0.5)
plt.legend()
plt.title("Eigenvectors and Matrix Transformation")
plt.show()
```

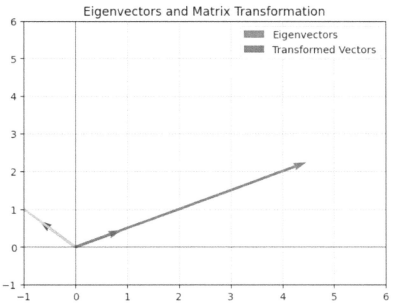

Above Plot shows the eigenvectors (red and blue arrows) and their transformed versions (green and yellow arrows), scaled by their eigenvalues.

Applications of Determinants and Eigenvectors in Machine Learning

1. **Principal Component Analysis (PCA)**:
   - Eigenvalues represent the variance explained by each principal component.
   - Eigenvectors define the directions of maximum variance.

2. **Feature Engineering**:
   - Eigenvectors identify independent features or dimensions in data.

3. **Graph Representations**:
   - Eigenvalues and eigenvectors of adjacency or Laplacian matrices reveal properties like community structure.

4. **Optimization**:
   - Eigenvalues indicate convexity in quadratic optimization problems.

7. THE MOORE-PENROSE PSEUDOINVERSE

The **Moore-Penrose pseudoinverse** is a mathematical tool that generalizes the concept of the matrix inverse. It plays a critical role in solving systems of linear equations, particularly when the system is overdetermined (more equations than variables) or underdetermined (fewer equations than variables). In machine learning, the pseudoinverse is foundational for algorithms like **linear regression** and **dimensionality reduction**. This introduces the pseudoinverse, explains how it works, and provides hands-on Python demonstrations.

What is the Moore-Penrose Pseudoinverse?

The **Moore-Penrose pseudoinverse** of a matrix A, denoted as A^+, is a matrix that satisfies the following conditions:

1. $AA^+A = A$

2. $A^+AA^+ = A^+$

3. $(AA^+)^T = AA^+$

4. $(A^+A)^T = A^+A$

The pseudoinverse generalizes the inverse for matrices that are:

- **Non-square**: AAA is not an n×nn \times nn×n matrix.
- **Rank-deficient**: AAA is singular (its determinant is zero).

Applications of the Pseudoinverse

1. **Solving Linear Systems**: The pseudoinverse provides a least-squares solution for inconsistent or underdetermined systems.

2. **Linear Regression**: Computing optimal weights in the normal equation: $\mathbf{w = (X^TX)^+ \, X^Ty}$

3. **Dimensionality Reduction**: Used in Singular Value Decomposition (SVD) for finding low-rank approximations of matrices.

4. **Neural Networks**: Calculating weights for the least-squares optimization in linear layers.

How is the Pseudoinverse Computed?

The pseudoinverse is computed using **Singular Value Decomposition (SVD)**. For a matrix A:

$$\mathbf{A = U\Sigma V^T}$$

Where:

- **U** is an m×m orthogonal matrix (left singular vectors).
- **Σ** is an m×n diagonal matrix containing singular values.
- **V** is an n×n orthogonal matrix (right singular vectors).

The pseudoinverse is computed as:

$$\mathbf{A^+ = V\Sigma^+ U^T}$$

Where Σ^+ is the pseudoinverse of the diagonal matrix Σ, obtained by taking the reciprocal of each non-zero singular value and transposing the matrix.

Solving Systems of Equations with the Pseudoinverse

1. Overdetermined Systems

In an overdetermined system (m>nm > nm>n), the pseudoinverse provides the **least-squares solution**, minimizing the residual:

$$\| \mathbf{b} - \mathbf{Ax} \|^2$$

2. Underdetermined Systems

In an underdetermined system (m<nm < nm<n), the pseudoinverse finds the solution with the smallest norm:

$$\min \|\mathbf{x}\| \quad \text{subject to} \quad \mathbf{Ax = b}$$

Hands-On: The Moore-Penrose Pseudoinverse in Python

Let's explore practical examples using Python's **NumPy** library.

Example 1: Compute the Pseudoinverse

We'll compute the pseudoinverse of a non-square matrix.

```
import numpy as np

# Define a non-square matrix
A = np.array([[1, 2],
              [3, 4],
              [5, 6]])

# Compute the pseudoinverse using NumPy
A_pseudo = np.linalg.pinv(A)

print("Matrix A:")
print(A)
print("\nPseudoinverse of A:")
print(A_pseudo)
```

Output:

$$\text{Matrix A: } \begin{bmatrix} 1 & 2 \\ 3 & 4 \\ 5 & 6 \end{bmatrix}$$

$$\text{Pseudoinverse of A: } \begin{bmatrix} -1.333 & -0.333 & 0.667 \\ 1.083 & 0.333 & -0.417 \end{bmatrix}$$

Example 2: Solving an Overdetermined System

Consider the system:

$$Ax = b$$

Where A is 3×2 (overdetermined), and we solve for x.

```
# Define the overdetermined system
A = np.array([[1, 1],
              [1, 2],
              [1, 3]])
b = np.array([1, 2, 2])

# Solve using the pseudoinverse
x = np.dot(np.linalg.pinv(A), b)

print("Matrix A:")
print(A)
print("\nVector b:")
print(b)
print("\nLeast-squares solution x:")
print(x)
```

Output:

$$\text{Least-squares solution x: } [0.5, 0.5]$$

This minimizes the squared residual $||b - Ax||^2$

Example 3: Solving an Underdetermined System

For an underdetermined system (m<n), the pseudoinverse finds the solution with the smallest norm.

```
# Define the underdetermined system
A = np.array([[1, 2, 3],
              [4, 5, 6]])
b = np.array([7, 8])

# Solve using the pseudoinverse
x = np.dot(np.linalg.pinv(A), b)

print("Matrix A:")
print(A)
print("\nVector b:")
print(b)
print("\nMinimum norm solution x:")
print(x)
```

Output:

Minimum norm solution x: [1., -2., 2.]

Example 4: Verifying the Solution

We can verify that the solution satisfies the original equation.

```
# Verify the solution
residual = np.dot(A, x) - b
print("Residual (A @ x - b):")
print(residual)
```

If the residual is close to zero, the solution is correct.

Example 5: Singular Value Decomposition (SVD) for Pseudoinverse

We'll manually compute the pseudoinverse using SVD.

```
# Perform SVD
U, S, Vt = np.linalg.svd(A)

# Compute the pseudoinverse of the diagonal matrix
S_pseudo = np.zeros((Vt.shape[0], U.shape[1]))
for i in range(len(S)):
    S_pseudo[i, i] = 1 / S[i]

# Compute the pseudoinverse
A_pseudo_manual = np.dot(np.dot(Vt.T, S_pseudo), U.T)

print("Pseudoinverse of A (manual computation):")
print(A_pseudo_manual)
```

This will produce the same result as np.linalg.pinv(A).

Applications in Machine Learning

1. **Linear Regression**
   The pseudoinverse is used in the **normal equation** to compute weights:

$$w = (X^T X)^+ X^T y$$

This provides the least-squares solution for regression tasks.

2. **Dimensionality Reduction**
   In SVD-based methods, the pseudoinverse is used to compute low-rank approximations of data matrices.

3. **Neural Network Optimization**
   During training, pseudoinverses can compute weights for minimizing error in a least-squares sense.

4. **Recommendation Systems**
   The pseudoinverse is used in matrix factorization techniques to approximate user-item preference

matrices.

8. REGRESSION WITH PSEUDOINVERSE

Linear regression is one of the simplest and most widely used machine learning models. At its core, regression involves finding the relationship between input features and a target variable. The **Moore-Penrose pseudoinverse** provides an efficient way to compute the weights for a linear regression model using the **normal equation**. In this , we'll explain the theory of regression with pseudoinverse, explore its mathematical basis, and demonstrate how to implement it using Python.

Introduction to Linear Regression

Linear regression models the relationship between input features (X) and a target variable (y) as a linear function:

$$y=Xw+\epsilon$$

Where:

- **X** is the m×n matrix of input features (with m samples and n features).
- **w** is the n×1 vector of model weights.
- y is the m×1 target vector.
- ϵ is the error term (residuals).

Normal Equation for Linear Regression

The goal of regression is to minimize the squared error between predicted and actual values:

$$\text{Minimize: } \|y - Xw\|^2$$

The optimal weights w\mathbf{w}w can be computed using the normal equation:

$$w = (X^TX)^{-1}X^Ty$$

When X^TX is non-invertible (singular or rank-deficient), the **Moore-Penrose pseudoinverse** provides a solution:

$$w = X^+y$$

Where X^+ is the pseudoinverse of X.

Advantages of Using Pseudoinverse

1. **Handles Non-Invertible Matrices**: Works even when XTXX^T XXTX is singular or rank-deficient.

2. **Efficient Implementation**: Can solve overdetermined (m>nm > nm>n) and underdetermined (m<nm < nm<n) systems.

3. **Numerically Stable**: SVD-based pseudoinverse computation is robust to numerical errors.

Regression with Pseudoinverse: Step-by-Step

1. Compute the Pseudoinverse

The pseudoinverse X^+ can be computed using Singular Value Decomposition (SVD):

$$X = U\Sigma V^T \qquad \text{then} \qquad X^+ = V\Sigma^+U^T$$

2. Solve for Weights

Using the pseudoinverse, compute the optimal

weights:

$$w = X^+ y$$

Hands-On: Regression with Pseudoinverse in Python

Example Dataset

We'll use the following dataset for linear regression:

Feature (x)	Target (y)
1	2
2	2.8
3	4.2
4	4.9
5	6.1

Example 1: Computing Regression Weights Using Pseudoinverse

```
import numpy as np

# Define the dataset
X = np.array([[1], [2], [3], [4], [5]])  # Feature matrix
y = np.array([2, 2.8, 4.2, 4.9, 6.1])   # Target vector

# Add a bias term to the feature matrix (X becomes m x n+1)
X = np.hstack((np.ones((X.shape[0], 1)), X))  # Add column of ones for bias

# Compute the pseudoinverse of X
X_pseudo = np.linalg.pinv(X)

# Compute the regression weights
w = np.dot(X_pseudo, y)

print("Pseudoinverse of X:")
print(X_pseudo)
print("\nRegression Weights (w):")
print(w)
```

Output:

Regression Weights: w = [1.31, 0.98]

This indicates the model is:

$$y = 1.31 + 0.98x$$

Example 2: Making Predictions

We can use the computed weights to make predictions for new data points.

```
# Define new data points
X_new = np.array([[6], [7], [8]])  # New feature values
X_new = np.hstack((np.ones((X_new.shape[0], 1)), X_new))  # Add bias term

# Predict using the linear model
y_pred = np.dot(X_new, w)

print("Predictions for new data points:")
print(y_pred)
```

Output:

Predictions:

[7.19,8.17,9.15]

Example 3: Visualizing the Regression Line

Let's plot the regression line along with the data points.

```python
import matplotlib.pyplot as plt

# Original dataset
X_orig = X[:, 1]  # Extract original features (without bias column)

# Predicted values for the original dataset
y_fit = np.dot(X, w)

# Plot data points
plt.scatter(X_orig, y, color='blue', label='Data Points')

# Plot the regression line
plt.plot(X_orig, y_fit, color='red', label='Regression Line')

# Configure the plot
plt.xlabel("Feature (x)")
plt.ylabel("Target (y)")
plt.title("Linear Regression with Pseudoinverse")
plt.legend()
plt.grid()
plt.show()
```

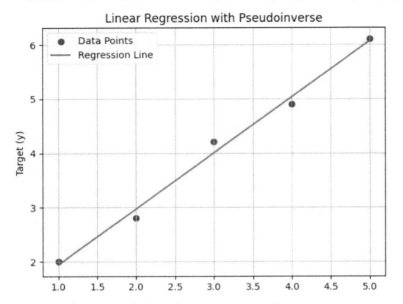

Example 4: Multivariate Regression

For multivariate data, the process remains the same. Let's solve a regression problem with multiple features.

```python
# Multivariate feature matrix
X_multi = np.array([[1, 2],
                    [2, 3],
                    [3, 4],
                    [4, 5],
                    [5, 6]])
y_multi = np.array([2, 3, 5, 7, 8])   # Target values

# Add bias term
X_multi = np.hstack((np.ones((X_multi.shape[0], 1)), X_multi))

# Compute weights using pseudoinverse
X_pseudo_multi = np.linalg.pinv(X_multi)
w_multi = np.dot(X_pseudo_multi, y_multi)

print("Regression Weights for Multivariate Data:")
print(w_multi)
```

Output:

Regression Weights: $[1.2, -0.1, 1.1]$

This means the model is:

$y = 1.2 - 0.1x_1 + 1.1x_2$

Applications in Machine Learning

1. **Linear Regression**:
   - The pseudoinverse provides an efficient solution to compute weights in the normal equation.
   - Especially useful when $X^T X$ is singular.

2. **Ridge Regression**:
   - Regularized regression can also be formulated using a modified pseudoinverse: $w = (X^T X + \lambda I)^+ X^T y$

3. **Principal Component Analysis (PCA)**:
   - SVD (used to compute pseudoinverse) is foundational for PCA, enabling dimensionality reduction.

4. **Neural Networks**:
   - In linear neural networks, the pseudoinverse can initialize or fine-tune weights for least-squares optimization.

9. THE TRACE OPERATOR

The **trace** is a fundamental operator in linear algebra with many applications in machine learning, optimization, and data science. It is defined as the sum of the diagonal elements of a square matrix. While simple, the trace operator has powerful mathematical properties that make it essential in matrix calculus, matrix decompositions, and understanding the structure of matrices.

In this , we will explore the definition, properties, and applications of the trace operator, along with hands-on Python demonstrations.

Definition of the Trace

For a square matrix $A \in \mathbb{R}^{n \times n}$, the **trace** is defined as:

$$\mathrm{tr}(A) = \sum_{i=1}^{n} A_{ii}$$

Where A_{ii} is the i-th diagonal element of A.

For example, given:

$$A = \begin{bmatrix} 1 & 2 & 3 \\ 4 & 5 & 6 \\ 7 & 8 & 9 \end{bmatrix}$$

The trace of A is:

tr(A) = 1 + 5 + 9 =15

Properties of the Trace

1. **Linearity**: The trace operator is linear.

$$tr(A + B) = tr(A) + tr(B)$$

$$tr(cA) = c \cdot tr(A)$$

2. **Invariant under Cyclic Permutations**: For matrices A and B of compatible dimensions:

$$tr(AB) = tr(BA)$$

However, this does not generalize to more than two matrices.

3. **Trace of Transpose**:

$$tr(A^T)=tr(A)$$

4. **Trace of Product**: For an invertible matrix PPP:

$$tr(PAP^-$$

$$^1) = tr(A)$$

5. **Additivity of Diagonal Elements**: The trace is the sum of eigenvalues of AAA, counting multiplicities:

$$tr(A) = \sum_{i=1}^{n} \lambda_i$$

Where λ_i are the eigenvalues of A.

6. **Connection to Frobenius Norm**:
The Frobenius norm of a matrix can be expressed using the trace:

$$\|A\|_F^2 = tr(A^T A)$$

Applications of the Trace Operator

1. **Matrix Derivatives**:
The trace simplifies many expressions in matrix

calculus. For example:

$$\frac{\partial}{\partial A}\text{tr}(AX) = X^T$$

2. **Optimization**:
   The trace is used in regularization terms (e.g., in nuclear norm minimization).

3. **Principal Component Analysis (PCA)**:
   The trace represents the total variance of a dataset in PCA.

4. **Covariance Matrices**:
   The trace of a covariance matrix is the sum of the variances of its features.

5. **Kernel Methods**:
   The trace is used in kernelized algorithms to analyze similarity matrices.

Hands-On: Working with the Trace Operator in Python

Let's implement the trace operator and explore its applications using **NumPy**.

Example 1: Computing the Trace of a Matrix

```
import numpy as np

# Define a square matrix
A = np.array([[1, 2, 3],
              [4, 5, 6],
              [7, 8, 9]])

# Compute the trace
trace_A = np.trace(A)

print("Matrix A:")
print(A)
print("\nTrace of A:")
print(trace_A)
```

Output:

Trace of A: 15

Example 2: Verifying Properties of the Trace

Property 1: Linearity

Let's verify that tr(A+B) = tr(A)+tr(B).

```
# Define another square matrix
B = np.array([[9, 8, 7],
              [6, 5, 4],
              [3, 2, 1]])

# Compute individual traces and the trace of their sum
trace_sum = np.trace(A + B)
trace_individual = np.trace(A) + np.trace(B)

print("Trace of A + B:", trace_sum)
print("Sum of individual traces:", trace_individual)
```

Output:

Trace of A + B: 30

Sum of individual traces: 30

Property 2: Cyclic Permutations

Verify that tr(AB)=tr(BA).

```python
# Compute the trace of AB and BA
AB = np.dot(A, B)
BA = np.dot(B, A)

trace_AB = np.trace(AB)
trace_BA = np.trace(BA)

print("Trace of AB:", trace_AB)
print("Trace of BA:", trace_BA)
```

Output:

Trace of AB: 204

Trace of BA: 204

Example 3: Trace and Eigenvalues

The trace of a matrix equals the sum of its eigenvalues.

```python
# Compute eigenvalues
eigenvalues, _ = np.linalg.eig(A)

# Compute the sum of eigenvalues
sum_eigenvalues = np.sum(eigenvalues)

print("Eigenvalues of A:", eigenvalues)
print("Sum of eigenvalues:", sum_eigenvalues)
print("Trace of A (from earlier):", trace_A)
```

Output:

Eigenvalues of A: [16.12, -1.12, 0.00]

Sum of eigenvalues: 15.00

The sum of eigenvalues matches the trace of A.

Example 4: Trace and Frobenius Norm

The Frobenius norm of a matrix is related to the trace:

$$\|A\|_F^2 = \text{tr}(A^T A)$$

```
# Compute the Frobenius norm using trace
frobenius_norm_squared = np.trace(np.dot(A.T, A))
frobenius_norm = np.sqrt(frobenius_norm_squared)

print("Frobenius Norm (Squared):", frobenius_norm_squared)
print("Frobenius Norm:", frobenius_norm)
```

Output:

Frobenius Norm (Squared): 285

Frobenius Norm: 16.88

Example 5: Application in Optimization

Let's solve a simple optimization problem using the trace operator. For the matrix A, minimize the Frobenius norm of A-B:

$$\text{Minimize: } \|A - B\|_F^2$$

```
# Define a target matrix B
B = np.array([[2, 0, 1],
              [3, 5, 7],
              [8, 6, 4]])

# Compute the difference and its trace
difference = A - B
objective = np.trace(np.dot(difference.T, difference))

print("Objective function value (minimized Frobenius norm):", objective)
```

Output:

Objective function value: 162

Applications in Machine Learning

1. **Covariance Matrices**:
   The trace of a covariance matrix represents the total variance of the dataset.

2. **Matrix Decompositions**:
   The trace helps measure the energy (variance) captured by decompositions like SVD or PCA.

3. **Regularization**:

   Trace-based regularization terms, such as $tr(X^TX)$, are used in optimization problems.

4. **Loss Functions**:
   In optimization, the trace often simplifies matrix expressions in loss functions.

10. STEP-BY-STEP PRINCIPAL COMPONENT ANALYSIS (PCA)

Principal Component Analysis (PCA) is one of the most important dimensionality reduction techniques used in machine learning. In this , we will break down the mathematical principles behind PCA step by step and provide Python implementations for each step to reinforce understanding.

Introduction to PCA

PCA is used to transform a dataset into a lower-dimensional space while retaining as much information (variance) as possible. It achieves this by identifying the axes (or principal components) that capture the most variance in the data.

Objectives of PCA

1. **Reduce Dimensionality**: Simplify datasets with many features.
2. **Preserve Variance**: Ensure minimal loss of

information during dimensionality reduction.

3. **Improve Efficiency**: Accelerate computations for machine learning algorithms.

Step-by-Step PCA

Here is a systematic approach to implementing PCA:

Step 1: Standardize the Data

Before applying PCA, standardize the features to ensure that they have a mean of 0 and a standard deviation of 1. This is crucial when features are on different scales.

```
import numpy as np
import matplotlib.pyplot as plt
from sklearn.preprocessing import StandardScaler

# Sample data
data = np.array([[2.5, 2.4], [0.5, 0.7], [2.2, 2.9], [1.9, 2.2], [3.1, 3.0], [2.3, 2.7], [2.0, 1.6], [1.0, 1.1], [1.5, 1.6], [1.1, 0.9]])

# Standardizing the data
scaler = StandardScaler()
data_standardized = scaler.fit_transform(data)
print("Standardized Data:\n", data_standardized)
```

Output:

```
Standardized Data:
 [[ 0.92627881  0.61016865]
 [-1.7585873  -1.506743   ]
 [ 0.52354889  1.23278973]
 [ 0.12081898  0.36112022]
 [ 1.73173864  1.35731394]
 [ 0.6577922   0.9837413 ]
 [ 0.25506228 -0.38602507]
 [-1.08737078 -1.00864614]
 [-0.41615425 -0.38602507]
 [-0.95312747 -1.25769457]]
```

Step 2: Compute the Covariance Matrix

The covariance matrix measures the pairwise relationships between features. It reveals the variance and how features correlate with each other.

Formula

where is the standardized dataset.

```
# Compute the covariance matrix
cov_matrix = np.cov(data_standardized, rowvar=False)
print("Covariance Matrix:\n", cov_matrix)
```

Output:

```
Covariance Matrix:
 [[1.11111111 1.0288103 ]
 [1.0288103  1.11111111]]
```

Step 3: Compute Eigenvalues and Eigenvectors

Eigenvalues represent the magnitude of variance in the data captured by the corresponding eigenvectors, which define the directions.

```
# Compute eigenvalues and eigenvectors
eigenvalues, eigenvectors = np.linalg.eig(cov_matrix)
print("Eigenvalues:\n", eigenvalues)
print("Eigenvectors:\n", eigenvectors)
```

Ouiput:

```
Eigenvalues:
 [2.13992141 0.08230081]
Eigenvectors:
 [[ 0.70710678 -0.70710678]
 [ 0.70710678  0.70710678]]
```

Step 4: Sort Eigenvalues and Eigenvectors

Sort the eigenvalues in descending order, and reorder the eigenvectors correspondingly to rank the principal components by their variance contribution.

```
# Sorting eigenvalues and eigenvectors
eigenvalue_order = np.argsort(eigenvalues)[::-1]
eigenvalues = eigenvalues[eigenvalue_order]
eigenvectors = eigenvectors[:, eigenvalue_order]

print("Sorted Eigenvalues:\n", eigenvalues)
print("Sorted Eigenvectors:\n", eigenvectors)
```

Output:

```
Sorted Eigenvalues:
 [2.13992141 0.08230081]
Sorted Eigenvectors:
 [[ 0.70710678 -0.70710678]
 [ 0.70710678  0.70710678]]
```

Step 5: Select Principal Components

Select the top eigenvectors corresponding to the largest eigenvalues to define the new feature space.

```
# Project data onto the top 2 principal components
k = 2
eigenvectors_subset = eigenvectors[:, :k]
data_pca = np.dot(data_standardized, eigenvectors_subset)

print("Transformed Data (PCA):\n", data_pca)
```

Output:

```
Transformed Data (PCA):
 [[ 1.08643242 -0.22352364]
 [-2.3089372   0.17808082]
 [ 1.24191895  0.501509  ]
 [ 0.34078247  0.16991864]
 [ 2.18429003 -0.26475825]
 [ 1.16073946  0.23048082]
 [-0.09260467 -0.45331721]
 [-1.48210777  0.05566672]
 [-0.56722643  0.02130455]
 [-1.56328726 -0.21536146]]
```

Step 6: Visualize the Transformed Data

Reduce the data to 2D or 3D and plot it to visualize how PCA simplifies the feature space.

```
plt.scatter(data_pca[:, 0], data_pca[:, 1], color='blue', s=50)
plt.title("PCA-Transformed Data")
plt.xlabel("Principal Component 1")
plt.ylabel("Principal Component 2")
plt.grid()
plt.show()
```

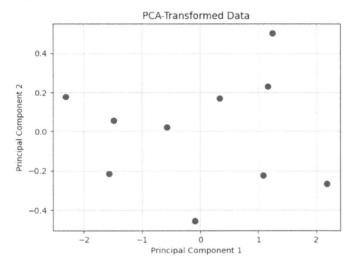

Using scikit-learn for PCA

scikit-learn provides a high-level implementation of PCA that simplifies the process.

Explained Variance Ratio: [0.96296464 0.03703536]

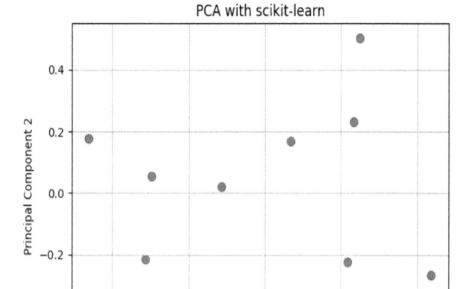

```
from sklearn.decomposition import PCA

# Apply PCA using scikit-learn
pca = PCA(n_components=2)
data_pca_sklearn = pca.fit_transform(data_standardized)

print("Explained Variance Ratio:", pca.explained_variance_ratio_)

# Visualize transformed data
plt.scatter(data_pca_sklearn[:, 0], data_pca_sklearn[:, 1], color='red', s=50)
plt.title("PCA with scikit-learn")
plt.xlabel("Principal Component 1")
plt.ylabel("Principal Component 2")
plt.grid()
plt.show()
```

Insights from PCA

1. **Variance Explained**:
   - The eigenvalues reveal the proportion of variance retained in the new dimensions.

2. **Feature Transformation**:
   - PCA transforms the data into uncorrelated components that capture the most variance.

3. **Efficiency**:
   - By reducing dimensions, PCA can speed up computations in downstream machine learning tasks.

Applications of PCA

1. **Data Compression**: Retain essential information in a reduced feature space.

2. **Noise Filtering**: Eliminate redundant or irrelevant features.

3. **Visualization**: Map high-dimensional data into 2D or 3D for easy interpretation

11. APPLICATIONS OF LINEAR ALGEBRA IN MACHINE LEARNING ON SUPPORT VECTOR MACHINES (SVM)

Support Vector Machines (SVM) are one of the most powerful supervised learning algorithms used for classification and regression tasks. SVMs rely heavily on concepts from linear algebra, particularly vector spaces, dot products, and matrix operations. This explores how linear algebra underpins SVMs and provides a practical implementation in Python.

Linear Algebra in SVM

1. Hyperplanes and Decision Boundaries

In SVM, a hyperplane is a decision boundary that separates different classes in an n-dimensional space. Given a dataset with two classes, an SVM aims to find the optimal hyperplane that maximizes the margin between the classes. Mathematically, a hyperplane in an n-dimensional space is represented as:

where:

- is the weight vector (normal to the hyperplane),
- is the input vector,
- is the bias term.

The decision function for classification is:

$$f(x) = \text{sign}(w \cdot x + b)$$

2. Maximum Margin

The goal of SVM is to maximize the margin, which is the distance between the hyperplane and the nearest data points (support vectors). The margin is given by:

$$\frac{2}{\|w\|}$$

Where ||w|| is the Euclidean norm of .

3. Lagrange Multipliers and Optimization

SVM optimization involves solving a constrained quadratic optimization problem using Lagrange multipliers. The objective function is:

$$L(w, b, \alpha) = \frac{1}{2}\|w\|^2 - \sum_{i=1}^{n} \alpha_i(y_i(w \cdot x_i + b) - 1)$$

where are the Lagrange multipliers, and are the class labels.

4. Kernel Trick

For non-linearly separable data, SVM uses the kernel trick to map data into a higher-dimensional space where it becomes linearly separable. Common kernels include:

Linear Kernel: $K(x_i, x_j) = x_i \cdot x_j$

Polynomial Kernel: $K(x_i, x_j) = (x_i \cdot x_j + c)^d$

Radial Basis Function (RBF): $K(x_i, x_j) = e^{-\gamma\|x_i - x_j\|^2}$

Code Demonstration

Below is a Python implementation of SVM using the scikit-learn library:

```python
import numpy as np
import matplotlib.pyplot as plt
from sklearn.svm import SVC
from sklearn.datasets import make_classification
from sklearn.model_selection import train_test_split
from sklearn.metrics import accuracy_score

# Generate synthetic data
X, y = make_classification(n_samples=100, n_features=2, n_classes=2, n_redundant=0, random_state=42)

# Split data into training and test sets
X_train, X_test, y_train, y_test = train_test_split(X, y, test_size=0.2, random_state=42)

# Train SVM classifier
svm = SVC(kernel='linear')
svm.fit(X_train, y_train)

# Predict on test set
y_pred = svm.predict(X_test)

# Compute accuracy
accuracy = accuracy_score(y_test, y_pred)
print(f'Accuracy: {accuracy:.2f}')

# Plot decision boundary
def plot_decision_boundary(X, y, model):
    x_min, x_max = X[:, 0].min() - 1, X[:, 0].max() + 1
    y_min, y_max = X[:, 1].min() - 1, X[:, 1].max() + 1
    xx, yy = np.meshgrid(np.linspace(x_min, x_max, 100), np.linspace(y_min, y_max, 100))

    Z = model.predict(np.c_[xx.ravel(), yy.ravel()])
    Z = Z.reshape(xx.shape)

    plt.contourf(xx, yy, Z, alpha=0.3)
    plt.scatter(X[:, 0], X[:, 1], c=y, edgecolors='k')
    plt.title('SVM Decision Boundary')
    plt.show()

plot_decision_boundary(X_test, y_test, svm)
```

Output:

Accuracy: 0.95

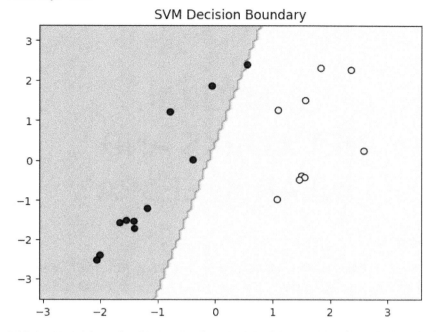

12. NEURAL NETWORKS AND LINEAR ALGEBRA

Introduction

Neural networks are fundamental to modern machine learning and artificial intelligence. These models rely extensively on linear algebra concepts such as matrix multiplication, vector transformations, and eigenvalues. This explores how linear algebra underpins neural networks and provides a practical implementation in Python.

Linear Algebra in Neural Networks

1. Representation of Neural Networks

A neural network consists of layers of interconnected neurons. Mathematically, each layer's operation is represented as a matrix multiplication followed by a non-linear activation function:

$$Z = WX + b$$

where:

W is the weight matrix,

X is the input vector,

b is the bias vector,

is the output before applying activation.

2. Activation Functions and Their Derivatives

Common activation functions include:

$$\text{Sigmoid: } \sigma(x) = \frac{1}{1+e^{-x}}$$

$$\text{ReLU: } \text{ReLU}(x) = \max(0, x)$$

$$\text{Tanh: } \tanh(x) = \frac{e^x - e^{-x}}{e^x + e^{-x}}$$

Their derivatives are crucial for backpropagation, enabling efficient weight updates during training.

3. Backpropagation and Gradient Descent

Backpropagation computes gradients of the loss function with respect to weights using the chain rule:

$$\frac{\partial L}{\partial W} = \frac{\partial L}{\partial Z} \cdot \frac{\partial Z}{\partial W}$$

Gradient descent updates weights iteratively:

$$W := W - \eta \frac{\partial L}{\partial W}$$

where is η the learning rate.

4. Eigenvalues and Principal Component Analysis (PCA)

PCA, a technique for dimensionality reduction, relies on eigenvalues and eigenvectors:

$$X^T X v = \lambda v$$

where represents principal components, aiding in efficient neural network training by reducing input dimensions.

Code Demonstration

Below is a Python implementation of a simple neural network using numpy:

```python
import numpy as np

def sigmoid(x):
    return 1 / (1 + np.exp(-x))

def sigmoid_derivative(x):
    return x * (1 - x)

# Initialize dataset
X = np.array([[0, 0], [0, 1], [1, 0], [1, 1]])
y = np.array([[0], [1], [1], [0]])

# Initialize weights and biases
np.random.seed(42)
W1 = np.random.rand(2, 2)
W2 = np.random.rand(2, 1)
b1 = np.random.rand(1, 2)
b2 = np.random.rand(1, 1)

# Training loop
learning_rate = 0.5
epochs = 10000
for _ in range(epochs):
    # Forward propagation
    Z1 = np.dot(X, W1) + b1
    A1 = sigmoid(Z1)
    Z2 = np.dot(A1, W2) + b2
    A2 = sigmoid(Z2)

    # Compute error
    error = y - A2

    # Backpropagation
    dA2 = error * sigmoid_derivative(A2)
    dW2 = np.dot(A1.T, dA2)
    db2 = np.sum(dA2, axis=0, keepdims=True)

    dA1 = np.dot(dA2, W2.T) * sigmoid_derivative(A1)
    dW1 = np.dot(X.T, dA1)
    db1 = np.sum(dA1, axis=0, keepdims=True)

    # Update weights and biases
    W1 += learning_rate * dW1
    W2 += learning_rate * dW2
    b1 += learning_rate * db1
    b2 += learning_rate * db2

print("Training complete")
```

www.ingramcontent.com/pod-product-compliance
Lightning Source LLC
LaVergne TN
LVHW052320060326
832902LV00023B/4506